W9-ADD-964

EASY MAGIC

by

Margaret Boothe Baddour

—for my teachers
Nancy King, Ruth Krouskup, William Harmon,
Ann Deagon, Calvin Atwood, Evalyn P. Gill,
Robert Pack, James Applewhite, and the rest.

*"We all write poems. It is only that the poets
are the ones who write in words."*
~ John Fowles

THIS BOOK WAS MADE POSSIBLE THROUGH A GENEROUS
GRANT FROM THE HANES CHARITABLE LEAD TRUST

ACKNOWLEDGMENTS ❧

The author wishes to thank the following for their assistance and encouragement in compiling this manuscript: my husband, Phil Baddour, publishers Ron Bayes and William Morris, good friends Winston E. Dees, Judy Goldman, Debra Kaufman, Janis McLendon, Mary C. Snotherly and Marsha Warren, and S. Tyndall Newall for the cover concept.

Grateful acknowledgment is made to the periodicals and anthologies in which these poems were first published:

Alamance Historical Calendar—Muse
Award Winning Poems of the North Carolina Poetry Society—The Baptising at Stony Creek
Blue Pitcher—Lost and Foundered, Several Strange Sensations
Crucible—A Shell from the Shell Man, About Zelda and Me, Second Mourning, The Decision
Four Hundred Years: Signs Along the Way—Morning Walks
Forum—Maizie
International Poetry Review—The Barnacle, Meteor Man, The Mad Hoer, What Color Is the Sun?, Smithsonian Album
Irene Leache Awards—What Color Is the Sun?
Lyricist—Copley Plaza Polka, Under the Influence, At Fontana Dam
A Murmuration of Purrs—About Zelda and Me, The Perfect Party
New North Carolina Poetry: The Eighties—These Geese
Pembroke Magazine—Birthday Revolution, The Day Dorothy and I Picked Up Pine Cones Because Women Have Always Borne the Burden, Sailing, They Lost Me
Potato Eyes—Here Where I Am Cold, On Our Passing
Prize Poems: National Federation of State Poetry Societies—Easy Magic
St. Andrews Review—Cello, The Gemstone Man, Letter to a Poet in the Schools, Lost on Buffalo Road
Southern Pines Pilot—Many of the poems printed here.
Stone Country—Land of Is

This End Up Postcards—All the Lovely Butterflies
Tug Boat Review—Double Entry Bookkeeping, Lines from Salter Path
Weymouth—Windows at Weymouth
Wind—Family Sketches, The Wild Magnolias

Some of these poems have been reprinted in the following anthologies:
More Than Magnolias, Writers' Choice, Women of the Piedmont Triad,
Poetry Under the Stars, Soundings, Our Words, Our Ways

© Copyright 1991 Margaret Boothe Baddour

ISBN: 0-932662-93-5

Printed by	Monument Printers & Lithographers, Inc.
	Verplack, New York
for	St. Andrews Press
	St. Andrews College
	Laurinburg, North Carolina
Design & Typesetting	Carol Tremblay
	Wordgraphics
	Wilmington, North Carolina
Cover Photo by	Brian Strickland

CONTENTS ❧

I WHIPPING AT THE AIR

II STARLIGHT AND STREETLIGHTS
AND SOFT DARKNESS

III HERE IN THIS PURE LOVE

IV A BLEND OF SUNLIGHT AND PERSISTENCE

I
WHIPPING AT THE AIR

Land of Is

My mother dries her blonde hair
like Mary Martin in *South Pacific*.
She always gets too much sun.
My father wears Bermuda shorts,
pulls a T-shirt over his dark chest.
They like Edgartown Beach.

To this present tense place, I bring
my past and helplessly watch it
spin onto the screen of island days
forgotten pictures. I should be
my parents' age—match their years
wrong for wrong and hurt for hurt—
not small and wide-eyed.

In this ever-present land, I perch
between them to eat scallops
on hard benches at the Black Dog.
Their friends laugh and talk around us
and I am safe. The future, a dark quarrel,
has blown out to sea.

The Wild Magnolias

Wild memories
of riding the black barked magnolias
me and Kitty Wallace
attacking the tree
gripping the trunk
to hoist up
and straddle a tangled limb
and ride feverishly
the wild magnolias.

My mother's wrath
at her blackened child
at the already dirty
urchin, Kitty
and the torn blossoms
strewn on the ground
booty from a mighty good time
upon the high seas
on the bucking bronco
riding the wild magnolias.

My genteel mother
my pale, light mother
caught me
riding the wild magnolias.

Old Buick Incident

When I climb on the old Buick's
glinting white hood
I can open my arms
flap off
and soar

          into

                  bird-blue sky
                  shimmery leaves
                  zig-zag clouds and

sunlight becomes starlight and
pollen is fairy dust and

                  KLONK!
                  the upside-down
                  ground.

The Perfect Party
~for Lou

Once
when green leaves hung mellow-golden
drunk with summer
when we shot marbles in the deep shade
on a smooth dirt circle
ran wildly through the paperboy trampled
hole in the hedge
when ragged robins and mint leaves
grew thick among the iris and the roses
and hummingbirds spun and nectared
in the trumpet vines:
there was an affair
a garden party
for a cat.

Little girls in organdy dresses
white and yellow
with puffy sashes
came, bearing gifts
        a rubber ball
        some choice salmon
        catnip
all wrapped in tissue papers
and curly ribbon.
There was tea
under the elm tree canopy
and birthday cake.
And the cat
though not at table
reigned supreme

preening himself
pouncing upon ribbon
sniffing the potent nip.

Then gleeful little girls
stuffed with cake
and draped in clover chains
played fairy queen
while he, the king,
with bristling whiskers
galloped in the grass
his coat black and white splotches
velvet
the green-eyed king
the whirling, darting king.

Once
when green trees hung drunk with summer
when slender mint leaves hid amid ripe roses
when dandelions, brilliant,
lay sprinkled in the grass:
there was an affair
a garden party
for a cat.

What Color Is the Sun?

My mother was an ash blonde
too smart for flowers.

But in the spring
we carried armfuls
gold-bursts of forsythia
and puffs of baby's breath
up the long drive

Clipped the stems
with neat scissors
for oriental arrangements
and in a house so dark
it echoed
there were always yellow flowers.

One springtime
she stooped
lithe and blonde
picked a daffodil
spoke clearly in my dream mind
of a daffodil's bright life
and withering death.

My mother
smarter than flowers
went up in flames
returned to yellow ashes.
What color, what color
is the sun?

Meteor Man

He was a lone star.
He hurtled back east from the promised land
hit these thirteen colonies
like a boiling comet
his blue eyes
firing shrapnel bits of the universe.

He was also a rich brown bottle of tonic
a medicine man from the prairie.

He was Rudyard Kipling
in the jungles of India and the Philippines.
Years after the war
he spoke highly of the Maharaja of Birdwan—
perhaps he really knew him.

For me he was vast
in the sky blue uniform.
Why one long-boned hand
could cover my whole small back.

And when I found myself
a tiny meteoric fragment of the man
I knew I could mold earths
in my hands
send suns twinkling from my feet.

They Lost Me

They lost me
before the funeral
though a great aunt
said she'd seen me just that morning
buckling my patent leather shoe.

> *It was my death wish*
> *killed you*
> *but they called it*
> *stomach trouble.*

I am sorry
dead little baby
but when my daddy found me
hunched in the crack
between their bed and the wall
(wearing my blue lace
funeral dress
and grinning dark and guilty)
he said
So there's my only girl.

> *Why did you come*
> *into this world*
> *with your strawberry hair*
> *and my face?*

And that afternoon
he took me up the street
to buy a pair of angel fish
and some balloons.

8

Family Sketches

Cousin Elizabeth
of the Romance languages department
swoops along
wild orange lily in her hand
under the crepe myrtles
toward the boxwood garden.
Interloping creature
but she's kin

Otelia Maria was a 'piscopalian
learning Greek and Latin underneath plantation trees
She never dreamed there'd be a Rachel Missouri
spittin' fire and brimstone
matin' with her offspring
Oh God, preachin' to the children
with gathering skirts, clutched bosom
kneelin' on her very Presbyterian knees.

Bamboo handled parasol from Hong Kong—
Aunt Otey appears
"Hah, Otelia! What a bag!"
pencil stub legs
knitting satchel purse
"Have a knock, Otelia. It's only good."
hat like a luminous red mushroom.

Waiting for the bands to play at half-time.

Esso

Cousin Carrie Osborne
Sister Osborne or
"Esso" upheld the internal revenue
under Woodrow Wilson, MacAdoo and Colonel Osborne
and received a turkey from the White House
each Christmas.
When Colonel Osborne left this world
with a band of angels
Sister Osborne upheld instead:
The Children of the World
The Keeley Treatment for Alcoholics
The American Indian
and various and sundry other charities
and do-good organizations.
And when she, too, left this world
bequeathed her closest relative:
a little golden harp
and two nodding Japanese figurines
not to mention yearly solicitations
from said organizations.
"Oh, well,"
Grandaddy used to say
"Ching Chiki Hai-O
Chuli Monki Rei."

Billie

Who is that waspish whoot-owl
holed up in the vacant room
tippling a bit
and nosing into every drawer?
Just Cousin Billie
back from Florida
and several luckless husbands.
Billie in her shapeless body
horn-rimmed glasses
wild hair.
Who does she think she is?
I claim no kin to her.
Why she lurks
an unpleasant shadow
with elephantine legs
and turned up bottle
holed up
in the vacant room.

11

Maizie

Her fat spreads on a high stool.
Oily—
hair like a steel wool scouring pad
wisping about a great
red mouthed center.

Queen of the rows of copper and tin utensils
that hang on the huge chopping table.
Queen of the yellow, copper, coffee
colored kitchen concubines
the Rubys, Loolas.
Queen of the lemon meringue pie
and the real string beans.

In the pantry it is cool
behind crates and cans
where I hide.

Near the great stove it is warm and rich.
The kitchen is a dark vacuum
a den, a cave
and Maizie is an ancient mother
not a mammy—

Big black maria
mammoth oiled red lipped
spread on a three-legged throne.

Aunt Maggie

When you come home
amber sunlight slants across the floor
and your big city scent fills the air.
We have fruit cake and egg nog
when you're here
because all the magic turns on for Maggie.
Maggie, you laugh divinely
gold and rust and Christmas red
come with you
and berries in your auburn hair
silver strings on the tree
bubbling lights so rare
we see them only once a year
when you bring them bubbling from the City
where the Yankees love you
think you are divine.

Do Not Go Gentle

The peonies, great white balls, bushed out,
reminding her of Summer, Grandfather, the South.
Their sweet scent filled her world, one room.
Her mind toured continents. She fought the night.
Opening soft white petals, the peonies
engulfed her, and she ravished them.

Second Mourning

Like an old aunt in lavender
I move along.
Light enough to bloom still
mauve enough to mourn
still regal, still holding violets
I accept the dawn.
Having shut my blinds
the necessary year
I change, now, from black to purple
become the shadow of light
the negative of darkness
enter my second mourning
more painful than the first.

The Mystery of the Sweater Trunk...

...begins with my mother, Helen,
astride a paint pony, her long neck bent
her gold hair aglint in the Texas sun.
My handsome father, looking like Tyrone Power
in *From Here to Eternity,* stands beside her
holding the reins. Her checked jacket, her shoes
in stirrups, the nape of her neck seem to move.
Do my eyes fill at seeing the old photograph
or does the past have a life of its own?
For these still people visit, in motion, my waking
and my dreams.

Containing the khaki-colored past, the white voile,
the black crepe, the burnt sepia of old photographs,
the metal sweater chest slept under my bed
for thirty years, its silvery lid dust-coated.
Last week I dragged it out, pushed open the lid
like a diver resisting water pressure and,
weak-kneed, lifted its people to the surface.
Not just the pretty blonde on a horse, the tall man
in uniform beside her, not just the same pair
dancing in Atlanta during World War II but pictures
from their own pasts: young people posing on porches
leaning against mantels, wearing —a vest,
a beaver coat, an evening gown. Not just
Depression folks but their predecessors
in little pony cart decked with flowers
or in ten-gallon hat, mounting an earlier
paint pony that rode the Chisholm Trail.
Now, at night, these antique people ride my dreams
chased by twisted images, warped signs.
To bring clear days and calm nights, I must
close the chest.

16

My baby, Helen, whose name means light, plops down
on the trunk of secrets. Full, like the Greek
Helen, of innocent guile, she finds a place to perch
and beats rhythmically the metal. Her brown bangs fly.
She kicks her corduroy legs, sings "Rock-a-bye-Baby."
Spreading her blanket, she covers the trunk's surface
 with her body.

All the Lovely Butterflies

All the butterflies keep bashing into my windshield
yellow ones and a few blue. Each wheels into view
from that blind spot inside my left brain, flutters forward
then careens into the glass. What form of hara kiri
forces such beauty at its peak to its demise?
The loveliest butterflies—that have passed, crossed, touched
possessed me this summer—perish before my eyes.

II
STARLIGHT AND STREETLIGHTS
AND SOFT DARKNESS

Easy Magic

I kissed a boy with gnarled teeth once
in Frankfurt
he was a soldier
and I felt sorry for him.
Nice to remember
nice for humility's sake.

I loved a drunk once
in Berlin
he staggered
and could barely sit upon his bar stool
but he was lithe and blonde
and I was just eighteen.
We ran whooping through the German streets
like banshees
whipping at the air like crazed egrets.

I sang poems on the beach
with someone dark and wiry once
sang loud and hard
till tide had come and gone
and we, encased in sand,
lay still
like grainy mummies.

Here in this pure love
a blend of sunlight and persistence
I ache to remember
the starlight and streetlights and soft darkness
the easy magic
in which I moved.

Zeus Poem

I need to write a Zeus poem
because Apollo shined on me today
and the golden boy pales
beside you.

You have more than rays—
why, you hold the lightning bolts
and Yeats said
you laid that girl.

I know you've been
both bull and swan
swan and swain
sainted and tainted.

Juggler of both worlds
you manage the mountain in the clouds
and still appear to mortals
in disguise.

Under the Influence

Let us have no more
perverting of legends.
make my Camelot story
as clear and clean as autumn's breath—
no sweetly drunken springtime, please.

Tell them there was Arthur
a bold and jolly Welshman
his blue eyes sparkling
sky drops of goodness
his pockets full of poems.

Tell them I was a Guinevere
who bathed in goodness
like a gold fish
in a sea green pond—
no wayward muse.

Tell them there was Mordred
a slug who should be salted
with my tears.
He bent our even lines
into an awkward triangle.

Let us have no more
perverting of legends.
Make my story clear and clean—
only a bit full,
slightly intoxicated.

On Our Passing

Bury me
in my black sequined lounging pajamas
on my old man's funeral pyre
piled high with poems.

Sing long
the fate of two
who, lost among the stars,
collided and found love.

Raise high
the funeral fire
to match our blazing flame
a toast to our desire.

Pile tall
the pyramid with poems
for after we are gone
the poems will live on.

Laugh loud
for in millennium's midst
Pharaoh's queen lies with
a sleek and silver star.

Here Where I am Cold

Here where I am cold
I think of Boston
how cold I was then
wearing a thin red suit
to look warm for you.
How we dined at the Copley Plaza
amid portraits of unknown
elegant people—
one with dark eyes in lace shirtwaist
looked like your mother, you said
"The moon, a velvet saxophone,
blows violent notes without you"
you said
and cried into an urn of escargots.

Here where I am cold
I sit with weights
like fish tanks
on my shoulders
my legs ache
and the IBM typewriter
raps hard on my brain.
Hard to look at sunlight
hard to smile
"You never laugh anymore"
they say
and treat me like a stranger.

I am a stranger to myself.
Having known only mimosa
and Queen Anne's lace
having known only the sun
and steaming black laps
I do not keen to this cold.

You came from slate.
You are sound rock, Mayflower blood
the only Yankee I could ever love
red-nosed, laughing
shooting silver sparks
at all of Boston
drowning linen tablecloths
with tears.

Here where I am cold
I wonder that Fall
comes back red and rioting
at all
chilling my veins
without you.

The Mad Hoer

And while you turn your back
the garden behind you
rises wildly from garage ashes:
blistering radishes split the ground
tight green tomatoes turn
to bloody moons and under mounds
the hard brown potatoes swell.

Run, boy, run from the mad hoer.
Tunnel your way to light
for at your back she hoes.
Her garden grows.

Squash blossoms eject snakes
crooked-necked and yellow
beans—fat, nubile—crawl
up your window into your dreams
corn horns erupt, tufted, at the rear
to ram your screen door
like a rhinoceros.

Run forward, Orpheus, lest
in turning back, your eyes arrest
and burn forever on your mind:
that girl curved at the hoe
brown and slick as a bottle
toes holding the dirt
hoe cleaving the earth.

Run from the mad, mad hoer
for at your back she hoes.
Her garden grows.

Lost and Foundered

In hemlocks, rhododendron
in apple trees, in small half-eaten
apples fallen on the grass—
his arms, his arms.

In mirrors, faucets, loose
in porcelain sinks, sharpened in ponds
misshapen in mountain lakes—
his slender fingers.

In crystal goblets, table cloths
in paper plates, in strings of pearls
in pale blue china, gold-ringed—
his wrists.

In river bends, in dripping moss
lost in holly, foundered in foxglove
found in iris —his arms
his arms.

Adrian Enters the Water

They are lowering the blue sailboat—
a technical matter for crane,
indifferent tow. The owner travels,
leaves business cards in his wake.
(I hold a cold, white card, wonder
what is the business of hands
that reach across board rooms, cup
smaller hands like nests.) They will
put in the boat without him, I guess.
A ritual missed.

But wait. That yellow streak.
A screech of cab. The golden domed
owner, rigged in rolled up slacks,
loosely knotted tie, flapping jacket,
wades into the basin to poke, dangles
belly-down from the dock to nudge
the boat which, long and slick, slides
into place and would easily glide out
over the Chesapeake Bay to sea...
but for the bow line.

Far away, I finger his business card.
Imagine him in the boat. Decide to slip
the bow knot. Riding the bow, I lean
leeward, laugh at ripples and gleams,
at the teak, porcelain, tufted gold
of man, boat and bay.

Several Strange Sensations

To peel the curled bark
from crêpe myrtle's arm
to touch that skin defies
almost defiles the sinews—
skin so pure, so fit
to virgin limb.

To cup the small cat Moco
to my head, to feel that
silken black mink, a cap,
hug my skull, take suck
from strands, drink sustenance
beyond milk.

To roll against cool porcelain
and smell shampoo, the only waves
a plastic curtain's shiver.
Bared bodies in bathtub, wet
without water, mummied forever
never come clean.

The Gemstone Man

A blue stone cracked with sand
the gemstone man wields,
twisting with pliers the golden wire.
The gemstone man —pink skin pocked,
eyes bulging, thick glasses—
rushes into my dream......
"The ring, the ring is ready!"
leaps, in little pants, wool cap
onto my spread. Only covers shield me
from that translucent face,
that oatmeal mouth. "I win.
Your name is 'Rumplestiltskin!'"
but he does not disappear.
"Rape, rape!" I cry. Still he wallows
until I wrench free from the dream......
I rise, put on my sodalite ring.
"These dreams mean nothing," I say,
afraid to face the day.

About Zelda and Me

When the boys call me
I still smell wisteria
sucking the red brick walls
wear white beaded dresses
hear crickets
carry tiny pink rosebuds
again
and drink champagne.

Didn't you know me
eons ago
before a cold autumn wave
slapped hard against my ear
stage-whispered that warning:
there will be red wine
and fireplaces
tears
and drafty rooms
silver laughter
and the knowledge of rotting leaves.

And do you know me now?
I am a mulatto mistress.
I sleep in a tight bed
with a black velvet cat
sleep until today is yesterday
is a white girl in a beaded dress
wanton, wild
champagne crazed
crying
"Good night, Jelly Bean"
to all the boys.

Christmas Wedding
~for Phil

Grandmother at the mantel, holding garlands
of pine, white roses, holly, must have felt
this way—all delicate in ecru lace
thin-veiled, her fine-boned hands so like
her own grandmother's in the portrait.
Her pale eyes could not guess my destiny—
that you, carrying frankincense and myrrh,
would bring me new worlds, salt seas that lap
at mountains, warm, dark-eyed people
who astonished even Alexander with their charms.
You are the charmer in my blue-eyed dreams
bringing them to life this Christmas
so I may tell granddaughter
that while men space-walked, you and I
were merging continents on earth.

III
HERE IN THIS PURE LOVE

In My Country

We cry
over small disasters
the twisted words
the wrinkled wings
the thick heavy summer night.

We cry
for fragile things
for mortal mimosa
immortal magnolia
the small thin call of the cricket.

Only the gravest words
bring slips of sunlight
silver laughter
quick endings
swift replies.

While small disasters
loom purple over Ocracoke
spread gray tears
through my country
and we cry.

Morning Walks

(Salem Academy~Founded 1772)

1967 ~ Mary Lee Speaks

My broad-beamed roommate from Maine
takes the circle shoulders first.
I puff, rush behind her, stretch
against this straight wool skirt,
bend hard into the April wind.
Beyond the circle, gravestones stand
in rows like rigid desks. (Miss Nowak
says: "Early walks made sunrise vigils
for people before us—the planters,
music makers, candle dippers, bread bakers
dressed in brown muslin, white caps,
knee breeches—who left us their ways.)
My roommate rounds her last lap of grass,
turns toward dining hall, head mistress,
Moravian manners that finish us
proper as pioneers.

1773 ~ Emma Speaks

At six-o'clock, I am the first soul astir.
My chance to view the garden solitaire—
mint, parsley, thyme, all good to eat.
Ah, but lavender for simple sweetness.
Come May, I'll pluck some for my pillow.
We laid this herbal garden in untilled soil
broke the earth with modest tools. Quite bold,
we pioneer in gardens as in lessons.
Today I feel free as any man, a leader
among women. Now the brass band tunes
in the cemetery, mixes bright with birdsong.
I pull the Easter air into my lungs
and circle the garden.

Lines from Salter Path

Only the ocean
is as big as I am.
I am bigger than most people.
Small towns split
like the Red Sea
to let me through.
I'm steely as a jaguar
slick as a shark
generous as a big breasted
Ashanti goddess.
Look out—
I am big as the ocean.
There's lightning in my touch
thunder in my step.
Only the foam knows me
when it runs up my large legs
and I laugh.

Whirring: At the Stonybrook Races

You are my general blur
my everyday doing, my alter-do
I take no time to think of you
Oh, whir ye by.

Two on a fence, a sun's shadows sift
while a grizzled old fellow
takes his hat in hand
and swoops a bow for the wholesome maiden
all rounded, supple, gold and pink—
I watch with you.

You are my alter-see, boy.
Whir ye by.

And the horses pound on.
Number 9 bolting, sweat and hysteria,
throws the jockey, who hurls his
whip—from here to the other end of hell.
It is that jockey's private hell
I feel with you.

You are my alter-be, boy.
Whir ye by.

Moon just a sliver and that single star
juxtaposed in a mystical sky
mystical me and mystical you
and a wild, balmy night in the knifing grass blades
knifing soft enough to cradle you and me
a sliver and a star for you and me
are you and me.

> You are my alter me
> my essence of essence.
> Don't you see what I see
> or near enough?
> Oh whir ye by

Nancy

Sometimes
when the wind is right
I see you gliding by, Nancy,
in a slick white convertible.
Men's eyeballs pop out
when you ride by
and their tongues hang down
on the sidewalk.
We all try to stop you, Nancy,
but you just keep riding by
tossing that yellow mane.

When the moon rides high and horny
blood sister
you rise in me laughing
with indigo eyes, great white teeth.

Sometimes
a tall girl flips round
a downtown corner
an Indian profile slips by
at the grocery.
I try to make them all you.

One night you sat up
by the moonlit window
stared strange and long
into the darkness.
Did you know then
how little time was left?

Sometimes
I see someone gold in white
whirling a tiny tennis ball so hard
it never comes back
and I try to call the ball back
but it just keeps whirling
the golden powerful arm
keeps arching up.

You were too much heat
blood sister
too much heat too close to earth.

Sometimes
I rush up close
to touch those big blonde girls.
They turn on me then
with every face but yours
and I take my hand away.

Garden Trilogy

I. Backyard

Dense with loveliness, my backyard,
and I created it, little Yahweh here.
Vermillion, magenta, coral, lavender
erupt through green, green, green—
every shade from the 100 Crayola box.
Ivy almost smothers the gray wall
to enclose me from all but rude sounds.
The gardenia-rimmed deck protects me.
On Sunday I survey my backyard.
And it is good.

II Vegetable Garden

The brightest spot, the lushest dirt
lie, alas, beside the poison oak
and Smoky, the neighbor's foul dog.
Lose your balance between eggplant
and peppers, and he will eat you, the way
he ate my cat, Dulcie, head first
through the fence rails. If he sleeps
in his weed-ridden lair next door
and you lose your balance, you might
die of poison oak. But come July
you pluck the richest apples from caged
vines—red as geraniums, tart
as lemons, round as the bloody moon.
Eggplant boats float in seas of sauce.
Peppers, radishes, cukes festoon salads.
Onions and squash divinely mash.
All fruits shoot from evil origins.

III Flower Garden

Groomed. Mulched. Meticulous. Rows
of zinnias, asters, snapdragons. If one
blooms, snip it with steel cutters to
propagate the rest. Yellow marigolds
trim the triangle but cannot restrain
the herbs: lemon verbena pours over
white pebbles, asking to be snipped for gin
and tonic. Oregano breeds like Italians.
Parsley, chives flower and go to seed
faster than we can eat them. Thyme
and basil beg to be dried. Mint
threatens to choke the garden. What
have I created? I cry, weak
from growing things and summer's heat.

Sailing
~for Mary Carleton Snotherly

Two town square giants, we survey at will
the tombstones, the torn streets, the rainbow flags.
We sail at will over sidewalks on bikes
and, landlocked, still dream of the moving sea.
Oh Beaufort, have you ever seen a more
be-ribboned girl than my thin golden friend
with no handle brakes, brown wicker basket
before her, salt lips set against the wind?

Only the wild ponies cannot reach us
in this town of characters who pervade,
through cracked plastic, our seedy room:
a tail-less tom cat, a drooling sailor
from the Joshua Slocum, a club-footed
guitarist from the Spouter Inn, the grim
bookstore man, the robust antiques dam,
the yachtsmen with lined faces, autumn hair.

All night a neon "Mike's Motel' invades
our flanneled sleep. In splintering September
light, we fight with visors the water's glare
share tarragon wine vinegar, tobacco
weavings, widows walks. Mosquitos seduce
us to the ancient graveyard to drain
our blood. We sail away, refuse to view
signs of the dead who clamored to Beaufort
by bicycle, by boat, and web-footed on land.

The Baptising at Stony Creek

Annie Dee touches one brown toe to the creek.
Cold, oh cold and pure rolls the water over stones.
White-robed, she waits, tallest of all the children
to go down, to go under. Here come the elders
a slammin' and a bangin' those tambourines. "Yes Lord!"
a shoutin' and a harpin'—"Now we shall gather"—
a dancin' and a chantin'—"Where bright angel feet
have trod"—and looking like a host of bronze angels
to Annie Dee who fears the creek will finish her
twelve years when Reverend Moses Jones lifts her to
paradise. "Now, my tall daughter of Israel,
wade with me into the water." Down he lays her
into the cold bed, calling for John the Baptist,
calling for Jesus. She submits to his hands
and sleeps, breathless as stones, for untold time.
"Rise and go forth, Sister Ann," cries Moses Jones.
She opens eyes and mouth to pine trees, clouds and sky
and sees that paradise looks just like home.

The Day Dorothy and I Picked Up Pine Cones Because Women Have Always Borne the Burden

The pine cones, closed up from rain like fists,
lie in threatening piles on this February fake
Spring day. I left them there last week for men
to gather. In my yellow plastic gloves, jogging suit,
scarf tails flying, I open bags and stoop. Up
walks Dorothy, says she enjoys doin' around outside.
Pine cones in bags, trash in barrow, we hoist the load.
Dorothy wears black cotton gloves. Pine cones prick.
She don't care. She must be six feet tall and brown
as Sojourner Truth, the abolitionist. But at sixty,
Dorothy acts modern in her jeans and a raincoat.
To think that after one hundred years, the gene banks
produced another Truth to pick up pine cones with!
Maybe she wonders that she and I, crossing the tracks
to sack containers, have lifted a language and a laugh.

At Fontana Dam

On the damp ground near my room sits
a dusk colored butterfly-moth
with clear eyes like mica. Overnight
it moves to the window screen, stays,
opens to full wingspan, slowly closes,
its fringed antennae alert, aloft.
I detect a tear on the right wing
but the fuzzed body does not decompose.
If I sent you this moth, packed in plastic,
would it spell you the hills, indigo mist,
the dank brook bed, ferns, spring water,
the lizard on the bridge (how I stopped
and he stopped, locked). Would it spell
the way these mountains enclose me like
the rim of a terrarium encases vegetation?
Here I am—caught in such lushness
as crept, primeval, over rich lava, the sky
a glass dome against which moisture rises.
Everything rising. Everything moist.

At the Boar's Head Inn
—Summer 1978

Yellow fledglings wag over the grass
after their fat mother.
These geese would rather waddle
than swim or even fly.
Hatched here, they paddle about,
never go north or south.
Out of twenty eight, only these remain.
The turtles ate seven, and one died,
under the mower, a fearful death.
How we trust these geese,
morning and evening, to give us poetry—
these and the round hills and willows.
In their microcosmic pond
green-necked mallards mix with common ducks
and the white swan floats
lissome, alone.

These Geese

Having dreamed them all year
we hesitate to see them, full feather,
perched on the bridge, dotting the pond.
But they never change, these geese,
only the swan has found a partner
and some miscegenation of Canada geese
with ducks produced a gaggle of misfits—
too long-necked to be one, too white
to be another. From this safe green place
we ponder silent Pound, tormented Poe
and all the small lost poets.
Plunging their necks below, the swans
lift triangle tails to fish for food.

We Dreamed It Snowed...

after Dylan Thomas

—for Philip and Mark

We dreamed it snowed...
sheets of it, grayer than our wall,
coated the pinestraw, the pavement,
the playhouse roof in the night
iced the paws and bellies
of dog and cats.

So delicious a snow...
that small boys, dreaming of vanilla
and cocoa, leapt the soft dunes
floated the tufted pillows
fingers pricking in their mittens
toes blue in their boots.

So quiet a snow...
we could hear the fields moan
the fat man with radish eyes
hold cold to himself like a muffler
while the fairy flakes shaped the pines.
We dreamed it snowed.

Blue Moon

She was born
on the evening
of a blue moon.
Earth's tides lurched
when she emerged
pink and slick
and singing
"La, la, la"
her legs taut
her arms a bloody threat
her eyes, that would be blue,
so black and daring.
Where did she come from
little Blue Moon?
Was she always
in the Eye of God?

Helen Amid the Asters

She picks her way along
tossing her brown bangs
eyebrows at V-formation
for concentration.
The asters mock her.
Each gauzy head bounces
back from her plump touch.
Only a few lie trampled
at her feet, testimony to
her two-year-old power.

Cycling on St. Simons
—Summer 1987

> *"It's the journey that counts."*
> *—Sam Ragan, NC Poet Laureate*

I pedal hard to reach the beach
past palmettos and live oaks.
Blown by Fords and Fiats
blared at by pickup trucks
I pump my own metal.
"Get on the bike path," a black woman yells.

Magnolia branches block the path
like highway robbers. I duck—
come up wet from garden hose.
Striped dress flaps, knees crack,
sweat drips on upper lip. I sail
through the village, past The Crab Trap.

At King and Prince Hotel, I lock
my bike, spread zinnia-covered towel,
slather the pale pink lotion.
Shall I lie, still as driftwood,
to salute the sun? No.
I fidget, writhe, dreaming of ferns,
of dangling vines, of treacherous bumps
I'll glide. I plot the return ride.

A *Shell from the Shell* Man

Bill hides in the Bahamas
rusty as a sunken frigate.
When he dives, he dives deep.
When he darts, he darts straight.
His nerves bounce off the balmish air.

And it's balm, balm, balm
in the Bahamas
yes, boy, it's balm.

Bare black ladies, regal as palms,
strut and bend and sway there
while suns unfold, rust gold,
in a thousand shells
wake in a thousand palms.

And it's palm, palm, palm
in the Bahamas,
yes, mama, it's palm.

Water falls cool
in the Garden of the Groves.
Water, shallow as skin,
runs everywhere
mixes calmly, like races.

And it's calm, calm, calm
in the Bahamas,
yes, man, it's calm.

Calm, as a lion, Bill brings forth
poems—charmed, speckled creatures
tiny, water pearled worlds in his palm.
A shell, from the shell man,
is a palmful of poems.

Yes, lord, of poems.

IV
A BLEND OF SUNLIGHT
AND PERSISTENCE

Portraits of Artists Who Escaped Their Childhoods Only to Illustrate the Poet's Nightmares

Evalynn the Printmaker:
"I grew up in Bear Branch
where, when you had a favorite pet
and it got hurt or sick,
you shot it and buried it
and got another pet."

And yet—the cat, Alice,
languishes before jade plants
dallies at drapes, reposes
in etching after etching
curled, arched, whimsical.

Elton the Painter:
"I couldn't bear the hog slaughter
in Ahoskie, but my daddy made me
watch and even help. He would shoot
'em in the head with a rifle.
Then my uncle would stab 'em
in the neck. Blood still stains
the farmyard dirt, I bet…"

And yet—the pig skates
pale pink with chartreuse sequins
on an indigo sea. Green vapors
rise around him. A faint smile
curves his acrylic lips.

Elton and Evalynn, Evalynn and Elton
illustrate the texts of my dreams.

Letter to a Poet in the Schools
—for Tom Heffernan

How was Smyrna?
Did they feel and smell
the way we planned?
Did the children build a giant
with beets and radishes for toes
to gallop him along?
And the cauldron—
did they eat from the cauldron—
witches' tears, frogs' tails, slimy slugs?
Did you rattle roasted nuts in their ears
and guide their fat hands
through the paper bag?
What about the words?
DID THEY MAKE WORDS?
Lazy as laughter, naughty as night
orange as apricots, plump as peafowl,
magic as mercury, quick as quagmires?
AND DID THE WORDS WORK?
Did they string up like cowries
pink and slippery and cool?
How was Smyrna?
What about the children?
Did they make words?

Lost on Buffalo Road in Misting Rain

A double rainbow flanks the steaming streets.
Horses straddle yellow fields. I bow through mist
to chestnut mare, to rainbow, to buttercups—
the way hummingbirds, enroute to Barbados, bowed
to e e cummings, whirring bejeweled in midair
tilting their tiny bodies to the great one.
I yearn to tell my laughing friends, safe
somewhere off this road. But I am lost.

The Barnacle

—for Evalynn Halsey

Good omen: that old beached boat
the Barnacle, hanging here in blue;
to find you in this strange place—
"Artist's Proof #2," wood cut,
the cartoon letters "Barnacle" raised,
like your eyebrows, in wry delight.
Forever taking notes for poems I might
write, I summon my muse—a merman
with froth hair, fins, barnacle tail
blowing a triton shell...

Bogue Sound: the sun, that fire globe,
threatens to crack the sound's glass
when it drops, slips instead over the rim,
leaving only mauve, lavender, teal blue,
amber in its wake. Seagulls startle
with their catlike sounds, wounded human
squawks. Even at night, through drapes
they cry, and I, wrapped in silence, dream.
The vaporizer knocks and knocks.
My throat, raped raw, calls: Come in!

64

Shackleford Banks: the merman sleeps
hoards rare sand dollars, driftwood,
eats seaweed, scallops, tender boys.
Winter barges pass seldom, churn gulls
to flight, the merman to emerge.
Behold! golden yacht girls, scuba women
at the Spouter Inn, basking in beer.
The merman ravishes them, naked.
Rumpled jerseys, blue jeans, wet suits
binoculars—heaped on the pier.

Emerald Isle: the merman beckons me
(foam circles his undefined lips)
hands me an oyster shell, purple,
shaped like a question mark.
"A snatch of skylarks!" he barks
and vaporizes in salt laughter
leaving blue hyacinths on the air.
I caress the barnacled pier
fondle the question mark, step over
rich brown gull droppings, into the sea.

Double Entry Bookkeeping

Let's be honest. For most people, accounting is boring.
Particularly for people engrossed in such heady activities
as changing society or helping people, balancing books
and preparing financial statements seems far less
important than delivering services and developing position
statements. After all, the most important thing about
money is getting it, isn't it?

—*The Grantsmanship Center News*
Issue 20, April-June 1977

I love your fat fingers.
If I were a cow
I would suck them.
If I were a duck
I would fuzz your forehead
yellow.
If I were a cougar
I would balance on your back.
If I were a black ledger
I would stand up on
double-entered figures
click my columns
and clog and clog and clog.

Dedicating the Grand Piano at the Art Center

—for Steve Hunter

I. Then there's the dream I have
about a finger slammed in a grand
piano: the pain comes chartreuse
like sound waves, but no sound,
only circling colors, throbbing thumb.
And I am again a small child
with brown bangs, screaming in the night
in a cherry blossom room, the finger
bigger than I am. The soundless slam
gongs.

II. Then there are dreams that stop.
Even the pain goes unremembered.
Waves change to smooth reflections...
a willowy man at a black piano
ripples the keys. The rain sings,
the colors, pure chords now,
tinkling wind chimes in sunlight.
The dark scream pulses, turns to roses,
to lavender iris, to cherry blossoms, to
songs.

Windows at Weymouth

A white rose flakes where it crept to bloom
inside on the window sill in a dark hall.
Far away—orange blossoms—sweet on the air.

Glass ripples, waves over the eighty-one
latticed places that enclose us, the arches,
bays, rectangles we look in, look out of...

Gothic panes reveal lavender, twin iris the color
of eyes. Yellow roses drape the old brick wall,
the stuccoed pool room, the pebbled lotus pond.

We want to be close to the iris, lavender tufted,
yellow throats—to think those paper-thin folds
enclose the ruffles, veins, fuzz of the full-blown ones.

Cherry trees, bowing in rows, grace the lawn
like skirts, like picture hats. A man named Green
keeps pushing back the forest, holding the woods.

In the holly tree a frantic brown cardinal
guards her rusted eggs. Red lover, green worm
painted against the pines—and the dogwood dying.

Eighty-one places from this and that—
the silver-haired one on the veranda, the one
typing in the garden. The ones we only know about

from sweaters left in closets, notes on mirrors,
saw in these sashed casements—shuttered, shuddered.
And we want to picture things as if seen

through windows. Two women sit on bricks
in sunlight, and it's terrible looking through
these windows at people crying...

Glass waves, ripples over eighty-one arched,
bayed, sashed, splayed, latticed places where we
look in, look out. We enclose them.

Cello

A cello sounds like a woman—
fallopian tubes opening and closing,
a blossom developing, something rich
like a magnolia, the color of cream,
stamen and pistil spattering the center—
piece with lush dust. A cello
is a mellow fruit—pomegranate—
the seeds spilling through the crack.
Lindsay hugs the cello between her knees.
Its pear-shaped body moans against
her thighs, laps at her lips.

Decision at Vandemere

Unspoken, the decision hung over us
like a domed bell. We embraced the gingham kitchen,
picked roses, between rainstorms, for little vases,
talked to village old folks, laughed a lot,
and on the pier, wept over poems by men
we did not know whose cruel words cut
the hot stars. "I cannot bear anymore," I said,
and in that one hour of sunlight you closed
the book and let the Bay River wind ripple you.
But the decision, now a graceful heron,
had entered you. I knew you would take wing.

Kay Wishes For A Camera

The secondary road, the kite
caught in the crotch of that old tree,
winter fields, wash on line, country church
(Kay sees through slant green eyes—
an architectural travesty),
pigs, plumped up as if painted,
before the white frame church,
ugly mother hogs, precious piglets
all pink sheen, silky and rounded.
Kay thinks to herself: the pigs
people the churchyard. She drives on,
wishes for a camera to record the scene.

Lois Dusts the Dining Room

Dust motes. Afternoon sun
splinters stained glass—
a vineyard orgy.
Emerald leaves spin.
Amethyst grapes spurt,
stain Lois's pale skin.
Her sky eyes refract
this splitting prism
the spirals and spades
of myriad rays.
She drops to the floor
to swallow the glow
that shatters the air.

Words to Run Your Tongue Over

—for Catherine McClain Armstrong

I. Working at the Gallery

Reds and yellows blare from silk screens
like trumpets at a bull fight.
On the right wall, colors cascade
green on blue down craggy mountains,
swirling, become browns and russets
mesas and deltas or the ocean's bottom.
On the far wall, the vermilion leaves
in a still life engulf the small round fruits
reach almost off canvas onto pottery
shelves where, in all their fullness,
fat vases, glazed indigo, shine.

Even as I write, I know these words
cannot convey the images I see.

I close my eyes, trace with my fingertips
the pottery ridges, the brush strokes
feel the canvas give when I push it,
stumble, across burlap, from canvas
to canvas, touching the brush strokes.
Yesterday you were born, perfect,
except for eyes. Today a blind man
calls here for tools to carve leather.

II Visiting the Cliffs

Traveling down Highway One-Eleven
I ponder art and nature. At the Cliffs
I lean far over the rail to watch
the river's curves carve the bank
one millionth degree more. Sediment
layers form rainbows of solemn browns.
A turtle, far below, dips and dives
struggles to shore. Down pinestraw paths
the mushrooms bloom, red and yellow.
Squirrels fairly fly from sycamores to oaks.

I close my eyes, try to imagine the Cliffs
without them. The musky pine odor,
the wisps, the tufts of Spanish moss, gray.
What is gray? The forest dense with noises.

I never saw a cricket till last year
yet his sound, lovely as honeysuckle,
means more to me than the ugly
dusk-colored creature on my threshold.

III Resting at Home

Ever think of this: the closed lids
that keep you from beauty, protect you
from ugliness...while your ears,
your fingertips, melt you with music
smooth you in velvet, sheathe you in silk.
You know black. As for the colors,
feel the sun's heat and know yellow.
Slide into grottoes for blue. For red,
listen to Ravel. For every shade
between—a smell, a sound, a touch.
For green, lie in wet grass. Purple—
a girl crying. Orange for fire places.
Pink for fuzz, like wild flowers, and sweet.

My gifts for you: words to run your tongue
over, to pummel, to caress, to whiff
sharply, like cinnamon...and my eyes
beginning, perfectly again, to see.

Smithsonian Album
—for Carrington at 12

As Oliver used to say:
"You can't take a picture
of the whole world."

You think I'll tell you how
to live harder faster more.
No. I am telling you now
the finest thing I know:
to live less
and love it more.
Give up the wide angle shots;
zero in on the minutia.
Pass up the cycloramas;
peer through the microscope.

One Ecuadorian whistle pot
means more than all the jungle bowls.
One long look at mirror sculpture
(the fountain shining in its eyes)
the wombat—half pig, half cat
the naked mole rat
the Green Dream Hand
the Spirit of Silk.
Not the whole world really—
just bits and pieces.

Caress the 3-Dness
of scooped chairs
like shell spoons.
Drink fountain water
with your mind:
swallow carefully the crest.
Feel the guards.
Like the Easter Bunny
or God
they see every thing.

Watch Madame under the canopy
hang on his every word.
Then Monsieur et Madame
beige and black
walk languidly away—
a speck.
A wind gust
and they're gone.

Save?
What will you save?
The gusty afternoon
a bit of laughter
the pin-prick of aching feet.
And what of "relief"
and Joan Miro
what of Rodin, abstract
the green mall
the water buffalo?

All these picture post cards—
learn to keep them
learn to let them go.

MARGARET BOOTHE BADDOUR

Margaret Boothe Baddour teaches Creative Writing for Barton College and Wayne Community College. She earned her MAT degree in English Education from the University of North Carolina at Chapel Hill.

A prize-winning journalist and radio commentator, she was an early organizer of the *North Carolina Writer's Network*. She is past President of the *North Carolina Poetry Society* and current secretary of the statewide *Arts Advocates*.

Her poetry has been published widely, and she has won the *N.C. Poet Laureate Award*, the *Writers Roundtable Award*, the *Irene Leache Memorial Award* and a *National Federation of State Poetry Societies Award*.